POWER MADE US SWOON

POWER
MADE US
SWOON

poems

BRYNN SAITO

 RED HEN PRESS | *Pasadena, CA*

Book design and layout by Abbey Hastings

ISBN: 978-1-59709-991-2
Library of Congress Cataloging-in-Publication Data

Names: Saito, Brynn, 1981– author.
Title: Power made us swoon / Brynn Saito.
Description: First edition. | Pasadena, CA : Red Hen Press, [2016]
Identifiers: LCCN 2015046622 | ISBN 9781597099912 (softcover : acid-free paper)
Subjects: | BISAC: POETRY / General. | POETRY / Asian.
Classification: LCC PS3619.A3987 A6 2016 | DDC 811/.6—dc23
LC record available at http://lccn.loc.gov/2015046622

The National Endowment for the Arts, the Los Angeles County Arts Commission, the Los Angeles Department of Cultural Affairs, the Dwight Stuart Youth Fund, the Pasadena Arts & Culture Commission and the City of Pasadena Cultural Affairs Division, the Ahmanson Foundation, and Sony Pictures Entertainment partially support Red Hen Press.

First Edition
Published by Red Hen Press
www.redhen.org

Acknowledgments

Some of these poems have appeared in the following publications, to whose editors grateful acknowledgment is made: *Adrienne Rich: A Tribute Anthology*: "Elegy with a Black Horse"; *Connotation Press*: "No History," "Reedley, CA, 1978," "In the Other World," and "Poem for the Shadow of an American Boy,"; *Lantern Review*: "Getting Clear" and "Dinuba, CA, 1959"; *Muzzle Magazine*: "Elegy with a Blue Wing"; *The Normal School*: "How to Tell the Truth," "What'll It Be," and "Intergenerational"; *An Online Artifact*: *Ghost Town Literary Magazine*: "Stone Returns, 70 Years Later" and "Alone in the Sierras"; *Poetry Northwest*: "One Day Dawn"; *poets.org*: "Like Any Good American"; *Revolution House*: "W.W. on How to Be Free"; *Southern Indiana Review*: "Stone in the Desert Camp, 1942" and "Stone Chorus: Manzanar."

My deepest thanks to the Napa Valley Writer's Conference, the Bread Loaf Writer's Conference, Kundiman, and Sierra Nevada College, whose gracious support contributed to the writing of this manuscript. A million thanks to Jason Bayani, Katherine Bourzac, Kris Brandenburger, Traci Brimhall, Tatyana S. Brown, Judy Grahn, and Valarie Kaur for reading and reviewing various drafts of the book. Much gratitude to recent workshop faculty, Kazim Ali, David Rivard, and David Tomas Martinez, for their astute feedback and critiques. I'm deeply indebted to Kate Gale, Mark Cull, and the entire Red Hen team for their continued support. To Maxine Hong Kingston, thank you for showing me the power of myth and story so many years ago. To my students and colleagues at California Institute of Integral Studies, Sofia University, and Kearny Street Workshop, I thank you for the dynamic learning communities we've created with poetry. To Roger and Chris Morimoto, thank you for your sustaining presence and generosity through the years. To the girls of Girl Camp, the condo crew, and the thunder cats of Napa, I'm indebted to your inspiring, life-saving spirits. Lastly, boundless appreciation to my parents, Gregg and Janelle Saito, and my sister, Leigh Saito: this book is a testament to our lives, our histories, our stories, and our love.

For Marilyn June Oh and Alma Nobuko Saito

CONTENTS

One

What'll It Be. 17

No History. 18

Reedley, CA, 1978. 19

Theory of Knowledge 20

Dinuba, CA, 1959. 26

In the Other World. 27

Poem Found Inside My Father 28

Getting Clear. 29

Two

Intergenerational. 33

Stone in the Desert Camp, 1942. 34

Displorations in the Desert. 35

Stone Chorus: Manzanar. 39

Stone on Watch at Dawn. 40

Stone Returns, 70 Years Later. 41

Lifting the Stone. 43

Three

Alone Time 47

Poem for the Shadow of an American Boy 48

Like Any Good American .50

What She Hears in the Shell 51

Elegy with a Black Horse 52

Ars Poetica 54

Directions for Falling 55

Four

How to Tell the Truth 59

One Day Dawn 60

Revision 61

Displorations Underwater 62

Night, New York 64

Wind Talk with Rilke Line 66

Five

Traffic 69

W.W. on How to Be Free 70

W.W. on the One Who Got Away 71

W.W. Remembers Her Sister 72

W.W. Writes a List 73

Six

Elegy with a Blue Wing 77

Notes. 79

Render voices to meet the weight of stone with weight of voices.

—Theresa Hak Kyung Cha

One

What'll It Be

Woman Warrior walks into a bar, sits down
says *You're welcome*
says *Hard rock*
says *So what, I know De La Soul is Dead.*
Woman Warrior orders whiskey sans ice, says
Want to watch me drink it, says
Down it I will in one to six seconds
with no one watching. From the forests crossing the rocks
above Woman Warrior's home town
sixteen hundred men
strapped with guns
took the territory in one to six and rested on the seventh.
She knew God liked rituals done in his stead
and so it was good.
Tethered as always to moonlight—
the high kind—Woman Warrior
fled the burnt town, arrived in the metropolis
found love, lost it, lost it again.
Now in the bar
bracing herself for the eye-full onslaught of broken lovers
Woman Warrior waits—
her head draped over her neck
her neck pouring down her back
her back like a poised metal sword.

No History

No history of suicide or insomnia
in my family   Histories
of bottles   fermenting blues
No history of oil   or industry
in my family   No legacy of leaning
over sunlit terraces   telling the masses
exactly what to do

History of luck and guns
in my family   scribbled in dust
Stone-colored snow-covered countries
in my family   Crows fleeing bodies
split   into two—

Body-as-country   Country-as-promise
Body-as-black-box-carrying-
a-promise   I begin   like an agent
to get it all down—

Histories of deliverance and delicate
walking around volatile
fathers   Histories of altars   Histories
of daughters praying   in moonlight
playing their hands in the streets
of new cities   Cities like saviors
for the bold   lucky few

Reedley, CA, 1978

My father's in the back of a pickup selling fruit
on the roadside with his nephews
in the fire-haze of summer.

Time before I was born, time before all of this
came into being—the kingdom of childhood, the girls'
education, the girls squandering girlhood

on baseball shards and mud gardens.
I want to imagine it all back, walk like a memory
up to the dusty truck, buy forty-five fat

and bloody melons as an act of advanced
apology. Me and the boys would talk about sports,
disparage the heat we love only

in secret. We'd watch my father haul box-loads
of vine fruit into the carriage,
wishing on lightning we could be that strong.

THEORY OF KNOWLEDGE

Many a doctrine is like a window pane.
We see truth through it but it divides us from truth.
—Kahlil Gibran

1.

My father carried his best friend's
daughter from the middle of the road
over to the side after the accident.
Walked all the way home to my mother
who stood pregnant at the front door
shocked by his blood-shirt. Morning
in the valley, California in the seventies,
quiet country roads. What changed
when Erin died? Wind through the bedroom
windows when I was a child, rustling
the curtains like underwater seaweed
and I wonder if it's her.

2.

When we were three and six my sister and I
walked away unhurt from the overturned
van after a drunk man driving swiped it.
It fell on our Grandmother, riding seatbelt-
less in the backseat, the crash shattering
her face bones. Copters circled
the LA night. My father rounded up a team
of strangers standing by to lift the van upright.
I was in the front seat when the impact
happened, window shattering like sun-fire
beside me, my father's sudden grip clawing
my left arm so I wouldn't fall into the glass.

3.

When I finally move to Paris, I will walk
everywhere. Close my fists around the iron
railing of my street-facing balcony,
sing into the sun as it rises. When I finally
move to Paris, I'll forget what I want
to remember, remember what I can't
forgive, write what I've never said aloud
to anyone. Perhaps I'll stop believing
in forgiveness as an operational concept
altogether. Sit in cafes with street-facing
seats and talk about redemption instead.

4.

Years later, still young. I spin
with my boyfriend in circles
on the freeway, black ice-
sponsored free ride,
Duran Duran on the radio,
Volvo intact afterwards
but totaled. Him crying
and me as the passenger
swallowing 8-balls of fear.
Rain coats the windows
and we wait. *Hungry like the wolf*
cries the song on the radio.
I'm on the hunt. I'm after you.

5.

Before I was born my mother's
oldest brother—
Now he's the ghost no one cries for.
He cries for us. He says
in the night: *You are brave*
like a stone is brave but all of your ideas
are glass windows.
I say: You didn't come up with that
on your own
and you know it.
He shrugs and smokes a cigarette.
He is so tall—is it really him? Firstborn
son of two worlds,
white T-shirt, bleached jeans, aviators even
in the dark hour. After a long
and tender exhale he looks
my way, saying: *You better get used*
to surrender.

6.

When I finally move to Paris, I'll think
about the stories, but I'll feel them
differently. Place them like quilt patches
across my chest and weave them strategically
around my body for warmth. In summer I'll sail
through the city on a boat, tearing off the blanket
by breathing, the heat and sun freeing me,
my skin, the new testament telling me I'm fine.

DINUBA, CA, 1959

Mother in the picture looking up
her eyes bright in black-and-white
white and frilled girl-dress
curled at the sleeves
bowl-cut hairdo.
Standing in the dust before the farmhouse
rehearsing her wonder
startled by bird flight
or surprised by the click of an old camera—
who knows.
I know who she becomes and why
though the *how* will escape me
continues to escape me
even in my terrible need to know.

In the Other World

You are young again   Your father has not gone
to the bar tonight   You do not have to find him   You do not
have to call around   asking for him
You're a girl-spark firefly   making your rounds across the field
at dusk   Dark descending   like a pool of freshwater
in a foreign country   in summertime   You ease into your life
You ease into the person   you were born to become
The shepherd on tour   with the guest artists   The carefree
candy collector   The cormorant downriver   dipping downstream

I see you in the other world   huddled over a candle
with a small group of citizens   dreaming wildly   eating
strawberries   sipping Red Stripe   You pace the night streets
pledging your survival   Singing   Sweeping away
the fliers after a long night   of calling out   You called out
for justice   You're fearless as a necklace   torn from the body
thrown to the wind

In the other world   history has not   circumscribed
your spirit   You're so close to freedom
you can taste it on the salt-winds   Your spirit is a songstress
occupying the sea

Poem Found Inside My Father

We lit the fire   Doug and I   beneath the boy in the tree
and laughed
and ran
and my father

    for which we were never

Camp made dad unpredictable

Watchtower, wire   Heart attack, two strokes

I could tell girls were different   Had two myself

They tip-toed around the garden
They weren't idiots

    they were never

The girls learned to run later   from different fires

Getting Clear

In the Great Central Valley
the hand of God lays flat on the land
as the light strengthens.
Night comes on like a curtain,
pulled by a flock of migrating birds.
I used to lie on my back
to watch them cross the sky
in an unbroken V.
How does a family learn to fly
like that? How do they know
the best seasons for leaving?

Two

Intergenerational

Woman Warrior is thinking about justice.
The moon out
and climbing the sky
reminding her of the slow light of progress.
Clocks line the banks of the frozen river.
They conduct time
tall and ticking while the river salutes the mystery
of ice. She skates across it
with a jar of honey
stacked on another jar of honey
stacked on another.
One hundred years later
and still she is skating, descended from the dark
river of women—women loving men
men loving bottled love
love like a cradle of needles—
mending, mending, mending.

Stone in the Desert Camp, 1942

Between the turtle rock and the crane rock
the children found me. I was shining
and smooth and silent about my secrets.
One day above me men with bony
shoulders came and built the barracks.
Then I couldn't see the sky for the rising camps
and I couldn't feel the winds, whipping
between the ranges; I couldn't see the ranges.
After a short time voices moved in
and I heard singing. Months later, dancing.
But mostly what caught me was the quiet,
concentrated chatter of elders:
How long before a working stove?
How to make a garden in this cradle
of limestone? How to coax a stream
from the highest of peaks in the freest of nations,
in this nation we sought for the blinding?
Some days no one heard the tears
but I felt them: they coated me like evidence
of a prior sea. I thought: this must be
how the humans felt when the rains
broke above them every two hundred days
and the waters for once didn't leak
through their roofs and they were happy.

Displorations in the Desert

Tuesday, late October. We wake at 5am to drive to the Manzanar National Historic Site—my mother, my father, and I.

I drive the first leg, to Weedpatch. My father drives the second. "Welcome to The Other Side of California," reads the sign at Lone Pine.

Bright yellow flowers, desert shrubs, Sahara mustard. The bluest sky. Mountains rise around us like sleeping, steadfast bodies.

In Manzanar, from 1942-1945, the U.S. Government incarcerated approximately 10,000 Americans of Japanese ancestry.

541 babies were born during the wartime incarceration.

Summer temperatures rose above 100 degrees. Winters were ice. People used tin can lids to cover knotholes in the floor when dust storms raged.

The earth outdoes herself, the earth sets you free, the earth says hello/goodbye.

Two barracks, reconstructed for the public. One watchtower—one of the eight guard towers, rebuilt. Otherwise, nothing on the grounds but plots marked for other ghost spaces: hospital, administration, gardens, cemetery, general store.

A white stone Buddhist memorial stands against the wind, Mt. Whitney in the background.

We drive around the site, stopping occasionally to get closer to the absence.

The earth gives you her best shoulder, the earth gives you the skin off her back.

My father's mother, Alma Teranishi, met her husband, Mitsuo Saito, in the camps. "She went in with one name and came out with another," says my cousin.

They were college-aged when evacuated. Sent to Gila River, Arizona—the location of one of two internment camps in the American southwest.

Alma said: "They packed us in like sardines," when describing the train ride from the assembly center to Gila River.

Alma said: "I used to lie and say I was Chinese." Meanwhile, my mother's mother, during the war, wore a button around town that read: *I Am Korean*.

The earth gives you the night air and nighttime breezes across a sleeping desert. The earth gives you the sweet elixir of sage and rain.

The Japanese have a saying: "Shikata ga nai." Nothing can be done about it. In the Manzanar gift shop, we buy a polished stone with the phrase engraved on it.

Next to the gift shop, in the museum, I take a photo of my father standing under a photo of a sign: Japs Keep Moving. This is a White Man's Neighborhood.

The earth is a traffic of broken hearts, the earth reminds you of your own death, which makes you glad.

The three of us eat dinner at the Bonanza Mexican Restaurant, visit the local pharmacy, spend the night at the Best Western Motel.

The earth listens when the ghosts forget you.

The ghosts forget to tell you they're going to die soon.

The night gives you stones, sand, voices, dreams. You take it all in, like a child. Your palms swallow everything.

You throw everything against glass and the glass shatters into sharp sunlight.

Sparks light the way.

The next morning, after the breakfast buffet, we walk for awhile in the bright desert light, then begin the drive home. My father drives the first leg; I drive the second.

In the desert, the ghost girls are free now, they play in the garden and give water to the yellow flowers with their cupped palms, though there is no water, there is the dream of water, which is enough for the girls and the flowers.

In the desert, the ghost girls live off their own ideas.

For awhile, I didn't have any ideas. I lived squarely in the world of brittlebush and Joshua tree, the Eastern Sierras rising like a shadow history.

I looked at my mother and I looked at my father, the three of us not saying much. We hardly said anything at all. The wind across the desert brought voices. We listened to the voices.

Render voices to meet the weight of stone.

I can't imagine—

I stood in the place of the barracks, arms out, idea-less. Reveling, for once, in the silence. I didn't run from the silence, the silence felt like freedom, like dipping my mind into a cool stream after days of walking the hard slope of a mountain.

Now the ghosts are everywhere. They are free to roam. We've unleashed them in their entirety.

Stone Chorus: Manzanar

What do you know about the broken cello
    burning in the field

with the China and the best linens?
    Why have you come here

with your brute singing, your pages with nothing
    not even lines

for a steady imagining? In the desert between the mountains
    the winds were luxuriant.

They were blue and carried rumors and little
    yellow flowers from barrack

to barrack and disease. We were surrounded
    I tell you. Power

made us swoon. The crowds of eyes
    never tricked us into false belief

we had no beliefs, we lived. Sometimes we dipped
    our fingers into coal

and dragged them across the night canvas
    but rare were such moments

of reflection. We ate the hours.
    The hours ate us.
        We forgot to transcend the holy.

Stone on Watch at Dawn

See the writer again
at the gate of memory?

The land cracks open with wind
and shots of rain.

She should drown her pages
in the sky, take to the ground
like a dogged gardener.

Turn the soil into something new—

Survive the past.

Whispers at the barbed wire
no longer suffice. What works is singing
from the cave of the self

where memories of knives
and clouds shaped like tiger faces

live together like children
unaware of their potential.

Stone Returns, 70 Years Later

The hotel's quiet as a teapot. The storms,
thirty miles east.

Her mother's sleeping beside her father, their bodies
barely touching. She drops me

into her left pocket
and slips into the night to stand in the field

and summon ghosts.
How to ask her to be so still

the desert flowers coalesce around her
like sky's chorus at dawn?

She can't. She paces the length
of the barrack blocks,

the dead weight of midnight like a sea
she can breathe in.

Her thumb and forefinger smooth my body
for certainty's sake but no matter—

I'm worn. I'm tired
of their histories. When I dream

I dream of silence so vast and expansive
it packs tight the space

beneath the canopy of stars.
It bears down like hail. It threatens

to swallow. What I have of a heart skips beats,
the long pauses between them

turning to ash.

LIFTING THE STONE

I open the Zen texts early in the evening.
The oak outside spirals wildly in the wind.
My sister calls from closer now and worry
for the world's forms rises in me
then subsides. Something or someone is singing
a new song scored in the style of silence.
I'm on the brink of becoming unrecognizable
to myself. Once I fought my way out
with words. Now breakers catch the salt waves.
The air is a miracle. Someone's come here
with a riddle—what is it? I'm an empty plane
waiting for flight in a field at dusk.
I am the field. Like the girl before me I go on
blindly, seeking a life with life at the center,
seeking a life with clarity sharp as a saint's knife
at the center. *Split the wood*, said the prophet
in the lost gospel. *Lift the stone. There I'll be found.*

Three

ALONE TIME

Woman Warrior wakes. Steps from the room's edge
into the center
stands naked in sunlight
reaches toward sun, moon, earth, air—
her arms like steel wings.
What can you do
to cure her of the one who left before sun-up—
his back like a thick bow
his future dark as a prodigal map
stretched across the ceiling?
Woman Warrior wraps herself in leather
runs to the river
five miles down
takes six long swims across it
calls out from the cold water to the absent maker
makes herself take zero breaths
when going under
for a long time.
When she comes up for air
the vultures circle high above her like living stars.

Poem for the Shadow of an American Boy

Never tell a woman you've got murder
        inside you, never let the bass overwhelm
                the treble, remember how your voice

has a history. Never write the coda
        before you find the hook, that is
                be as good as you can when standing

by a burning car with a girl inside it
        and a boy on the roadside making wishes.
                Be good to the doves cooing nocturnes

through your window, though I know
        you'll want to kill them, I've seen
                that kind of rage, it makes my mouth

fill with ash. One day you'll wake wondering
        where your mind went, what it held to
                when the body shook, why the body

betrays the spirit's quest over and over.
        Swaths of time like cut ribbons of seawater
                to thrash around in. Silent sky at dawn.

The muscle in your chest beating
        2/4 time against the breath's 4/4.
                On such mornings if you're lucky

the one beside you will be breathing
      in half-notes, composing with her shoulders
        or composing with his shoulders

the prelude to your redemption.

LIKE ANY GOOD AMERICAN

I bathe my television   in total attention   I give it my corneas
I give it my eardrums   I give it my longing
In return I get pictures   of girls fighting   and men flying
and women in big houses   with tight faces   blotting down tears
with tiny knuckles   Sometimes my mother calls
and I don't answer   Sometimes a siren   sings past the window
and summer air   pushes in   dripping with the scent
of human sweat   But what do I care   I've given my skin
to the TV   I've given it my tastes   In return   it gives me so many
different sounds   to fill the silence   where the secrets
of my life   flash by like ad space   for the coming season

What She Hears in the Shell

Unsure on the shoreline and moving
like secular shaking—she.
She on the shoreline, unmoored, unmet,
met and unmet by the buttery ocean
with better believers—we.
We make a world for her

hoarding horses under starlight
and starlight overseas seeming mad
and seeping seaweed messages.
*Make might by launching long kites
into sky-orbits. Make right
by releasing kites.* Messages like that.

We make messages like that
in seaweed strands, plastered
to a man's back. We move madly
over watersheds and the heads
of nonbelievers and no one sees.
In the sea of her beginning,

blood rust and roving mud
loved her body into being, we believe.
So render us real, why don't you?
Risk twisting your arrows
into ash, then relax—more magic
in the mid-life than you think.

ELEGY WITH A BLACK HORSE

for Adrienne Rich

You tended the earth with your unquiet rage
waiting for rain the way some women wait
for a man's dry fist to stop its music
against the oak door. When you departed

for the heartland, the weather of America
knocked on your bones—inland winters and salt-air
from the coast made claims to your muscles
and your mind. Poetry and time were of no match

for you: your words outgrew the airless rooms
of boxy stanzas the way a black horse stays true
to her body's desire for the quickest winds.
On the day you died, I was pulling artichokes

from the sweet soil, scraping my teeth
against the cupped leaves until the hearts lay bare
like rope knots. I took from the field house
Grandfather's shovel; I loaded the florets into

the flatbed and drove and drove until the valley
disappeared into the slopes of Pacheco
and the sea arrived like a testament of blue,
the color draping every dream I've had

since you departed. What will we do
with the many question marks you've made for us
in sticks along the dark trail? In the bright light
of madness, I turn to her and I turn to her

and nothing perceivable changes, save a voice
calling back from the shell of another.
We are women, it says. *We travel together.*
This is what you never failed to let us forget.

Ars Poetica

after Muriel Rukeyser

Were you right all along—is the poem
a neutrino or starlight disappearing
across impossible seas? What
was your moment of proof—
standing on the ship with the other
outcasts, speaking in tongues? Breaking
through the stained glass image
of Mary, breaking color and sound?
Sometimes I wander down Broadway
with my head in my chest, my hands
tucked under opposite armpits.
I see you in the south—your body
on the line for justice, your body
in the northern woods crafting outrage
and joy into art's energy. *Everything
we had heard*, you said, *everything
we had heard and some of all we loved
and feared has begun to be acted out.*
Sum of staircases and labyrinths,
temples and sunlit fields. Water—
the gift of form, given to the poem
in torrents—physics finding its limits
and exploding into strings.
When I meet you on the page
there's a tingle in my wrists, a luminous
body of light occupying the spine's
column. And I believe it has begun.
It has begun to be acted out,
cry the blind girls in the choir,
the steeple in ruins, the ruins singing.

Directions for Falling

You, young. Waiting for thumbnail moonlight, married
to the sea. When sweet long love presents itself
wear the colors of your bio-region, make prayers
for west coast rain. Wait for two women in identical
floral dresses to light your laughter-face, *then* enter
the restaurant, lit with the energy of your own potential.
Take cab kisses and grass-stained jeans. Take mannerly
distance for delicious letters written with an ear
for the epic. Keep tending to the bodies that help you
remember: his listening eyes, her sister-love in Mexico
where you, in fuller moonlight, were re-ensouled.
In one iteration, you float heart-up beneath an oak tree—
you and the tree breathing a fuller sequence.
In the other, love is a hippo devouring everything.

Four

How to Tell the Truth

Woman Warrior knows when the wrong thing
is spilling from her mouth
like a bowl-full of wet dead leaves
or crust on the underside of a rusted red wagon.
She sees herself sometimes
talking with strangers in bars
and boardrooms
and back rooms of bars, saying *I feel okay*
do you feel okay,
now that I feel okay
and have said so?
Last year this time Woman Warrior took a plane
to a winter mountain
where monks with swords
sliced through falling snow.
This, she thought, *is the meaning of clarity.*
This is the way
to stop spilling mottled leaves on everyone I love.

ONE DAY DAWN

One day dawn I wake remembering something that never
happened to me—not me, not my girl-body,

not my father holding me down.
Days later, Venice Beach at dusk, and dolphins

in the middle distance:
me telling Valarie everything again: *I'm afraid of my mind,*

I'm afraid of being alone
with my mind

and its memories—
what kind of fear is that? I ask the sand, the sea, the sea-winds,

the gold from a sun-now-gone gracing Val's face.
As if the mind had a mind of its own.

As if the mind were a lion—capable of taking you down
by the river, where silt turns to blood-salt

where stones begin their speaking
where stories roam like wild bees—

You are here, says Lee. *Not where you feared you would be.*
Here, says Lee. *Not where you feared*

so take up the pen, press it to the veins—
draw bloodlines in cursive, like smoke.

REVISION

But what is the poem *about?* asks David,
the two of us around a table in northern Vermont—
cocktail hour, not a bar around for miles.
How I believe what I can't remember, how memory
is the engine of myth, how beer cans and laughter-
kings thread through the bloodlines of a common
American girlhood. I don't know whose story
has taken up residence in my body, what ghost.
David takes my pen, crosses out the entire poem
on the table before us, the one we've been staring at
for an hour. *Say that then,* he says to me. *Say it.*

Displorations Underwater

At fourteen, I painted the walls of my bedroom dark blue.

Suburban flesh, quiet midnight, maple leaves and whistles in the trimmed yard.

Girlhood was a cord. Blue was the color that could cut it.

I was haunted by a low voice rumbling out from the TV screen, telling me to take from the kitchen the sharpest knife and cut along anywhere calling out for renewal.

I had a vision of my grandfather ascended and dangling over a grape field, strangled by a belt.

What is that? I said to my mind. Hooked to nothing, he floated like an O'Keeffe skull over a desert landscape.

During girlhood, I learned to keep time by the swelling and receding of weird visions.

I learned to go inward.

Some of me stayed there, straying. Wandering the ragged foothills at dusk.

Decades later, oaks curling over a black-bottom pool, curious as guardians. California sunlight like seaweed, streaming. I release thoughts in bubbles. My body recognizes itself as the sea creature it once was.

Displore—to explore your own despair.

Move around in it, underwater fish-woman.

In the mental health hospital—early March, age twenty—people move slowly, swimming through the space like billowing bodies in a restless sea. I meet a girl curled over a guitar singing a Radiohead song, fishhook fashioned to the corner of her mouth, line taut to the sky.

All matter must go through pain and then it is released.

After my release: nights in major cities, walking near the river, telling the stories without which we would vanish into orbit. *Then, the demons fled and I gained a second self. I gained a witness.*

San Francisco, Amsterdam, Seoul, New York. Bridges lit with streetlights and smokers. Waters rushing below us, cooling the mind. *Then, I survived.*

NIGHT, NEW YORK

Throw a stone into the sky high enough
so it will not come back.
—Yoko Ono

Summer in the terrible
> city of terror
>> summer of relief

eating us like thunder
> summer of uncut shame.
>> You wail onstage

like quaking light
> I gesture with flesh
>> towards a future self

I make a wing of girlhood's ether
> and release it.
>> In art's aftermath

you're quick to compose
> like a lean glass
>> holding boiling water.

Radial movement minus gloss
> and apology.
>> Woman of worlds

and uncovered nations.
> I don't have a language
>> for what the body can do

when free and alone
        in a wide room
                with broken light

but good God I want one.
        In the questionable dawn
                the sun rises like a gear.

I go in to it with a handful
        of stones, cut
                by invisible lightning.

Wind Talk with Rilke Line

Some days I try to see
outside of myself. I try to stand
outside of myself
but the wind says,
Don't let yourself lose me.
The wind says, *Let me wrap myself
around your body.*

I say, *What I want is to be a ghost
in the world of knowable things—
that cold unknown.*
The wind replies by carrying me over
a pine-spotted mountain
where smoke coils rise. My life
was never my own.

Five

TRAFFIC

Woman warrior when stuck in traffic
sings love songs, screams, screeches her wheels
across the lost metropolis
puts locks on certain memories
to survive. She has nothing
to say to you
she has everything
to say to you
she sees you in the next car—
forehead pressed to the steering wheel
stereo blaring
sweeping your mind with your eyeballs.
You're a full-blown adult now—
blind as a hubcap to the unseen world.

W.W. on How to Be Free

Go to the ends of the earth / girl / go like a leopard chasing her longing / go like the grasses grown and cut and blowing / over the valley by autumn fire-winds / Go away from the valley / girl / go to the city / Go like a fighter / with gold ore precision / with penny-like pain / with plenty of power / Please ignore what you can / girl / the growls in your absence / the men with their ice blocks / melting in arms / the men with their mine-field hearts / The women like me / whistling wisdom into your spine / learn to lie to survive / girl / learn to outlast the flame / learn the art of surprise

W.W. on the One Who Got Away

I wanted to / lie down beside him so I / took the sharpest / knife I could
find / I placed it / between our bodies in the long grass / the grass greedy for
moonlight / the moon greedy for sky / me with my desire dancing / on the
knife-edge / We turned to face each other / half of each / body / submerged
in shadow / half in the light / while the knife gleamed / All I couldn't bear
to lose sat loose at my back / blue figures resting / with shrouded faces /
folded hands / and fireflies / When you're a warrior it doesn't / matter / you
must always / wake at dawn

W.W. Remembers Her Sister

Denizens in a country of longing / We were last-standing / and streaked / with moonlight / We were eating our own defeat / I didn't account for the horse power / the bullets / the dawn-stream of light / the flags stitched in blood across beaded foreheads / Before they arrived / I called for my sister / I commanded her / to behead me / so the enemy would be / deprived of the glory / What she did in my name / haunts her like two unclosed eyes / beaming in the seas / of her dreams / What she did in my name / binds her to me like a shadow / in this life / and all unnamed / lives to come

W.W. Writes a List

Candy / Cholera / Collect calls from drunk loves / Drugs / Dragon memo-
ries / Memories like stones / Dragging memories like stones through south-
ern deserts / Though I like the desert / Though the desert does me good /
the silence cutting like comforting sword-winds / Father / Fire / Figurative
fear / Finding echoes in the ether / Tracing echoes in the ether / ever testing
this weather / ever tending to the desert / though the desert does me good
/ and I know I have to leave it / like leaving a lullaby sung to a womb / We
are wandering women / Warriors wanting / Warriors wishing on the dark
of the tomb

Six

Elegy with a Blue Wing

When the time arrived for revolution
        our hands bloomed white with carnations.
             The man with the steel

and the man with the machete
        stripped sugarcane from stalks
             and sat like children to gnaw the fiber.

The sun gave up the earth.
        The world as we knew it ended not
             in fire but in the midnight darkness

of a winter road. We accepted this.
        A land without light excited us.
             We used our tongues to taste the embered air

and our shoulders with no armor
        to know the wind's direction.
             Now we walk the length of the forest

without you, though some nights
        you're beside us and again we're showering
             in summer light and again we're lying

our bodies across a field of dead leaves
        in autumn. I wish I could show you
             how good I've become at counting to ten

by tapping my fingers against hip bones
       when rain pounds the wickered dark.
             I know how to breathe underwater now.

I know what's beyond the wish we had
       for a changed world. In my solitude
             I'm free to remember you.

Some days the memory aches
       like spice on the heart's drum.
             Some days it's a blue wing, lifting.

NOTES

"Displorations in the Desert": Manzanar was one of ten internment camps built across the United States during World War II. In total, nearly 120,000 Isei (first generation) and Nisei (second generation) Japanese Americans were incarcerated, two-thirds of whom were American citizens. Ultimately, none were charged with treason or espionage. The U.S. government, in 1988, decreed that the wartime incarceration was based on "race prejudice, war hysteria, and a failure of political leadership."

"Directions for Falling" is for Lisa Wells.

"One Day Dawn": The line, "You are here, not where you feared you would be," is from Lee Herrick's poem, "Salvation."

"Wind Talk With Rilke Line": "Don't let yourself lose me" is from Rilke's *Book of Hours: Love Poems to God.*

Biographical Note

Brynn Saito is the author of *The Palace of Contemplating Departure*, winner of the Benjamin Saltman Poetry Award from Red Hen Press and finalist for the 2013 Northern California Book Award. *Power Made Us Swoon* is her second book of poems. Brynn co-authored with Traci Brimhall *Bright Power, Dark Peace*, a chapbook of poetry from Diode Editions. Her work has been anthologized by Helen Vendler and Ishmael Reed; it has also appeared in *Virginia Quarterly Review*, *Ninth Letter*, *Hayden's Ferry Review*, and *Pleiades*. Brynn is the recipient of a Kundiman Asian American Poetry Fellowship, the Poets 11 award from the San Francisco Public Library, and the Key West Literary Seminar's Scotti Merrill Memorial Award. Recently, Brynn served as the Kundiman Writer-in-Residence at Sierra Nevada College. Born and raised in Fresno, CA, Brynn currently lives in the San Francisco Bay Area.